The Joy That Is Jazzy

Written by Shawna Boudreaux

Illustrated by Stefanie Williams

This book is dedicated to Ed

ISBN   978-1-7361117-8-9   (Hardback)

All rights reserved. No part of this publication may be reproduced, or transmitted in any form or by any means, including photocopying, recording, or other electronic or mechanical methods without the prior written permission of the publisher. For permission requests, solicit the publisher via the email or physical address below.

SG Boudreaux

PO Box 12936

Lake Charles, La. 70612

Printed in the USA

Sgboodro2@yahoo.com

www.SGBoudreaux.com

Copyright © year 2022 by SG Boudreaux Publications.

All rights reserved. All images are trademarked and are the property of the publisher.

Hi, meet Jasmine, or Jazzy as we have always called her. Jazzy was diagnosed with Encephalopathy when she was around five months old. Encephalopathy is where part of the brain does not work at all. Doctors always told us that Jazzy would be unable to walk, talk, hear, see, or do anything for herself. She can do all of those things and much more. Jesus took care of Jazzy when she was a baby through all the prayers that went up to heaven for her from so many people all over the world. Jazzy is a real miracle and brings so much joy to everyone she meets. She is a very special person. And whether or not you have learning disabilities like Jazzy, you are just as special as she is. Jesus loves you just as much.

Let's hear what Jazzy's friends from all over the world have to say about what Jazzy means to them, and how they see Jazzy and her wonderful, joyful, personality. The descriptions that follow are actual descriptions from others, and some words are big.

Jazzy is a friend to all, a special soul is she.

She will make you laugh and smile, and as happy as can be.

Her many friends from all around, from church, from camp, and homeschool too;

They all love Jazzy very much, and this is what they want to tell you.

Jazzy is a spunky girl, bubbly, sparkly,
   and enlightening,
Her adventurous spirit is contagious,
   and her joy is so inviting.
Her imagination is inspiring, she's unique,
   and entertaining.
She's wondrous, wonder-filled, infectious,
   informative, and often quite intriguing.

She flits from person to person, like a butterfly that makes people smile.

Her honesty and pureness of heart, truly makes her a special child.

She lives her life in "ALL CAPS"—which simply means to the fullest.

She draws you in with her smiling eyes, she really is the coolest.

She's the keeper of childhood memories,
   and loves with inspiration.
She's a kaleidoscope of beauty,
   like light seen through a prism.
The childhood wonder we try not to lose,
   a reminder of times long forgotten.
She's inclusive, comical, accepts all as her friends,
   and will never leave you lonesome.

Her neighbor friends all say such things as well; they love her simple view of life.

She's different in the best sense of the word, and has little in the way of strife.

She's a morning rooster caller, and a songbird talker, mimicking the nature she hears.

She's enchanting and brave, distinctive, outgoing, unique, interactive, and fierce.

She's amazing, brilliant, joyful, and fun, like the brightest star in the sky.

She loves to play with whoever is willing, she certainly is not shy!

She's helpful and willing, protective and caring, a stranger she never meets.

She's a problem solver, energetic, imaginitive and sassy, to play with her is a real treat.

She likes to cook, bake, and decorate; her pumpkin painting is fabulous.

She loves rocks, bright colors, books and beads, to her they are all so precious.

She draws her chalk art in the sunshine, in rainbows, and flowers, and dragons.

Her dragons she loves above all else, and rides them around in her wagon.

Her therapist friends say Jazzy is this:
    jovial, compassionate, and whimsical.
Each week she would show them a new dragon friend,
    and often would say things quite comical.
She tries to work hard for her therapist friends,
    though sometimes, they wear her out!
Working on buttons, and reading, and spelling;
    but doing new things makes her proud.
She knows she must work to do things that are hard,
    she knows what they tell her is true.
Doing these new things gets her all excited.
She likes to learn things that are new.

Bathtime is hard since her right hand is weak, her fingers are just a bit tight.

Holding the soap with the rag is hard since her fingers don't want to work right.

Washing her curly hair by herself is tough, because she has so much!

She tries her hardest to do things herself, but she always needs help with a hairbrush.

Her dragon doctor friends say she's a fierce dragon keeper; her all-time favorite toys.

She loves things with wings, loves to dance and to sing, and also likes to make lots of noise.

Her new trampoline is her new favorite thing, she bounces her dragons with power!

The sun casts her shadow as her arms spread wide, and they soar through the air for an hour.

She loves the beach and the water too, the seashells make her smile.

Her skin gets all pruny, her eyes and nose swell, because she has swum for a while.

She swims like a fish, and will do so all day, till mom tells her it's time for a break.

She sits down to rest from her pool-time play, and asks for some chocolate cake.

She is joyful, creative, playful, imaginitive, innocent, and just likes to run.

A truthsayer, enchanter, a bringer of joy, though, sometimes things aren't always fun.

Sometimes she gets scared when things aren't what they seem.

She's sometimes unsure she can do certain things.

She doesn't like thunder, but the rain is okay.

Lightning is scary, but she knows it goes away.

Her many aunts, uncles, and cousins, have all of this to say:

She's a priceless, innocent, sweetheart, who inspires them all to pray.

She is spiritual, a miracle, and a blessing, sent straight from heaven above.

She's a tapestry woven in color so bright, an illuminating gift of love.

She makes you feel loved and included, and as special as can be.

And her presence and smile can light up a room, just like a Christmas tree.

Her Grandpa and Grandmas say she is unique, unstoppable, determined, and a learner.

A wonder-filled playmate so full of whimsy, a friend, a helper, and a server.

She roller skates, ice skates, rides her scooter too, and dances with joy and abandon.

She likes dragons, seagulls, birds, and bats, and is a fierce and a constant companion.

Her sister says Jazzy is focused on things, like those that she wants to do.

She loves movies, music, coloring, and art, and thinks her sister's Jeep is cool.

She loves to take pictures, make videos, blow bubbles, play games, and listen to tunes.

But her most favortie thing is to go for a ride with sister, while they croon.

Her brother says she is stubborn, and hard to push around.

She definitely knows her own mind, and can really stand her ground.

Her brother makes her laugh at his silly goofy ways.

When he jokes, and pokes, and picks on her, she knows he only plays.

Her mom and dad say she is wise, and a teacher, and always such a joy.

Life is definitely more interesting now, ever since Jazzy was born.

She often makes them laugh and smile, and surprises them with all that she knows.

Her great big heart for others, is always what she shows.

So take heart my young friend when you
 find yourself down, God loves you with
 all of His heart.
He made you with love, a divine plan in mind,
 so listen to what He imparts.
When you're feeling quite sad and life has
 you down, and you're unsure of just what to do.
You can talk to Jesus, for He's always around,
 and His love will help see you through.

There's one more thing that I will say,
   the truth the Bible states.
It says Jazzy is made in God's image,
   and that He makes no mistakes.
You too are a child of God,
   long before you were born.
A blessing, a gift, an inheritance,
   the future, a true reward.
This is how God sees Jazzy,
   and it's also how He sees you.
She is incredibly and wonderfully made,
   and you are too!

About the Author

SG Boudreaux is a stay-at-home mom who has home-schooled her three children for the last twenty years. Two have graduated, and her youngest is an eighteen-year-old, special-needs child. She and her husband of twenty-seven years live in the country, in a small rural area, just outside of Lake Charles, Louisiana. She was born in West Virginia, lived in Florida for many years before moving to Louisiana with her mother and youngest sister. She married a local boy and has lived there ever since. She loves the culture, the people, the sense of community, and definitely the wonderful Cajun food. You can find out more about her and her books on her Facebook, Instagram, or Twitter pages, or on her website at   https://www.sgboudreaux.com

Her previous series of books are MG and YA genres and are clean-reading, fiction, epic fantasy, and time-travel. You can write to her at the address in the front of the books.

About the Illustrator

Stefanie Williams is a self-taught artist, specializing in acrylics and watercolor portraits. She is married to a career Army Officer which takes them all over the US. They are currently settled in Virginia. She is active on Instagram and Facebook as @the_tattooed_christian

Other non-fiction books by Shawna Boudreaux:

My Journey to Better Health - a self help, encouragment, information book.

Clean-reading, fiction, epic fantasy, time-travel novels by Shawna written under the penn name SG Boudreaux:

The Peregrination Series - five novels, fiction, epic-fantasy, time-travel;

The Zanchier Series – three novels, fiction, epic-fantasy;

New series to come in 2023 – The Lightwalker Series – three books – more information soon to come.

You can find more about her works on her website at https://www.sgboudreaux.com

Her books can also be found on Amazon, B&N, Goodreads, Bookbub, and many other venues, and can be sourced anywhere IngramSpark and Lightning Source Books are sold.

www.ingramcontent.com/pod-product-compliance
Lightning Source LLC
Chambersburg PA
CBHW041109210426

43209CB00063BA/1860